From Egg to Adult
The Life Cycle of Mammals

Heinemann
LIBRARY

Mike Unwin

H **www.heinemann.co.uk/library**

Visit our website to find out more information about **Heinemann Library** books.

To order:

☎ Phone 44 (0) 1865 888066

🖹 Send a fax to 44 (0) 1865 314091

🖥 Visit the Heinemann Bookshop at www.heinemann.co.uk/library to browse our catalogue and order online.

First published in Great Britain by Heinemann Library, Halley Court, Jordan Hill, Oxford OX2 8EJ, part of Harcourt Education Ltd. Heinemann is a registered trademark of Harcourt Education Ltd.

© Harcourt Education Ltd 2003
First published in paperback in 2004
The moral right of the proprietor has been asserted.

Editorial: Nicole Irving and Georga Godwin
Design: Jo Hinton-Malivoire and AMR
Illustrations: David Woodroffe
Picture Research: Maria Joannou and Lizz Eddison
Production: Séverine Ribierre

Originated by Dot Gradations Ltd
Printed and bound in China

ISBN 0 431 16860 1 (hardback)
07 06 05 04 03
10 9 8 7 6 5 4 3 2 1

ISBN 0 431 16867 9 (paperback)
08 07 06 05 04
10 9 8 7 6 5 4 3 2 1

British Library Cataloguing in Publication Data

Unwin, Mike
From egg to adult: The life cycle of mammals
571.8'119
A full catalogue record for this book is available from the British Library.

Acknowledgements

The Publishers would like to thank the following for permission to reproduce photographs: Ardea/Augusto Leandro Stanzani p. **8**; Ardea/Chris Brunskill p. **17**; Ardea/Francois Gohier p. **20**; Ardea/Jean-Paul Ferrero p. **14**; Ardea/M. Watson p. **5**; Bruce Coleman/William S. Paton p. **7**; Corbis pp. **10** (top), **19**, **21**, **24** (bottom); FLPA/ Minden Pictures p. **27**; FLPA/Jurgen & Christine Sohns p. **25**; FLPA/Minden Pictures p. **16**; FLPA/R. P. Lawrence p. **12**; FLPA/Sunset p. **4**; Getty Images pp. **24** (top), **26**; Nature Picture Library pp. **11**, **13**; NHPA/ Ann & Steve Toon p. **6**; NHPA/Laurie Campbell p. **18**; NHPA/Martin Wendler p. **10** (bottom); Oxford Scientific Films/ABPL Photo Library p. **22**; Oxford Scientific Films/Ben Osborne p. **23**; Oxford Scientific Films/Liz Bomford p. **9**; Oxford Scientific Films/Mark Deeble &Victoria Stone p. **15**.

Cover photograph of the new-born elephant, reproduced with permission of Oxford Scientific films.

The Publishers would like to thank Colin Fountain for his assistance in the preparation of this book.

Every effort has been made to contact copyright holders of any material reproduced in this book. Any omissions will be rectified in subsequent printings if notice is given to the Publishers.

Contents

What is a mammal?   4

How are mammals born?   5

What do baby mammals look like?   9

Who looks after baby mammals?   11

How do mammals grow up?   15

How do mammals find a home?   17

When do mammals have babies?   22

How long do mammals live?   25

Fact file   28

Mammal classification   29

Glossary   30

Find out more   31

Index   32

Look but don't touch: many mammals are delicate and some may bite or kick. If you see one in the wild, do not approach too close. Look at it but do not touch it!

Any words appearing in bold, **like this**, are explained in the Glossary.

What is a mammal?

All mammals have a backbone and are known as vertebrates. Their bodies are supported by **endoskeletons** and they breathe air through their **lungs**. Mammals are also **endothermic**, which means that their bodies turn food into energy to keep them warm. All mammals feed their babies on milk and care for them as they grow up.

A pangolin looks more like a reptile than a mammal. Underneath its hard, shiny scales, it has a soft furry belly, like most other mammals.

All sorts

There are over 4600 different **species** of mammal, including mice, cats, horses, monkeys and even us humans. Most are furry or move on four legs, but some are different. Whales are mammals that live in the oceans. Like fish, they have smooth, hairless bodies and fins to help them swim. Bats are mammals that catch their food in the air. Like birds, they have wings to help them fly. We human beings walk upright on two legs.

How are mammals born?

A female mammal produces tiny eggs, but she does not lay them, as birds or reptiles do. Instead, they are **fertilized** inside her body by the male's **sperm**. A fertilized egg develops into an unborn baby, called a **foetus**. The foetus grows inside its mother. In most mammals, it gets food and **oxygen** through the mother's **placenta**.

Waiting to be born

A foetus stays inside its mother's womb as it develops and grows bigger. This period of time, while the baby is waiting to be born, is called the **gestation period**. The length of a gestation period varies between one mammal and another. For African elephants it last 22 months – nearly two years. For mice it only lasts three or four weeks.

A safe place

When she is ready to give birth, a female mammal finds a safe place. A polar bear digs her den in the snow. A hare makes a soft hollow in the ground and lines it with her fur. A grey squirrel makes a nest in a tree.

A polar bear gives birth deep inside her snow den, where it is much warmer than outside.

Some female **social mammals** leave their group or herd to give birth in a secret place. The female fallow deer does this. She then introduces her baby to the herd when it is a few weeks old. Others, such as elephants, give birth right in the middle of the herd. Here, its mother and all the other members of her family can protect the calf from danger.

When an elephant is born, other members of the herd get very excited and crowd around the mother and baby to watch and help.

Headfirst into the world

Most baby mammals are born headfirst. A new-born human baby has a **skull** that is flexible, because the bones have not yet joined together. This means that its big head can be slightly squashed during birth so that it squeezes more easily out of the mother. After a few weeks, the baby's head hardens into a more rounded adult shape.

New-born hedgehogs have their spines hidden underneath the skin, so they do not hurt the mother during birth. A few hours after they are born, the spines emerge and start to grow.

Hiding the evidence

Once a baby mammal is born, the placenta is no longer needed, so it comes out of the mother. A used-up placenta is known as afterbirth. Some female mammals, such as gazelles, bury or even eat their afterbirth, so that its smell does not attract **predators** to their babies.

How many babies?

Some mammals, such as rhinos, give birth to just one baby at a time and then wait a few years before having another. Most smaller mammals have many more babies and give birth more often. Female hamsters have **litters** of about ten babies and produce two or three litters each year.

Born underwater

Unlike most mammals, a baby dolphin is born tail-first. This helps it to get oxygen from its mother while it is being delivered underwater. As soon as the baby is born, it makes straight for the surface to breathe its first oxygen from the air.

A new-born dolphin weighs up to 20 kg – about one tenth of its mother's weight.

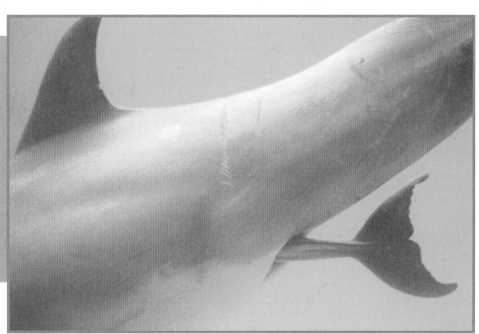

Population explosions

When there is plenty of food, Norwegian lemming females have a litter of five to eight babies. After only four weeks, these babies can have litters of their own. The number of lemmings increases very quickly. This is called a population explosion. However, with many new mouths to feed, the food is quickly used up. Many lemmings die, and breeding slows down among those that remain.

What do baby mammals look like?

Many new-born mammals, including cats, mice and rabbits, are completely helpless. They do not look much like their parents, since they have little or no fur, and they cannot walk or even see. Human babies are among the most helpless of all. We cannot even sit up until we are at least six months old.

New-born grey squirrels are naked, blind and have no teeth. Fur starts to appear after two weeks, and they first open their eyes after one month.

Ready to go

The new-born babies of **prey** animals that live in the open, such as giraffes, look just like their parents – only much smaller. They are covered in fur and can see clearly as soon as they are born. At first they are a little wobbly on their feet, but within minutes they can walk and very soon they can run. This helps them to keep up with their mother and escape from **predators** such as lions.

A mother giraffe uses her long tongue to lick her new-born baby clean.

Keeping out of trouble

Some mammals are born with patterns that disappear as they grow older. These patterns make up a **camouflage** that helps them to hide from danger. A baby tapir has spots and stripes. These look just like the pattern of light and shadow on the **rainforest** floor where it lives. When she wanders off to search for food, a female tapir knows that her baby is well hidden.

It is hard for predators such as jaguars to spot a baby tapir because of its camouflage markings.

Who looks after baby mammals?

Because new-born mammals cannot look after themselves, they stick close to their mothers all the time. A kangaroo stays inside its mother's **pouch**, a baby anteater rides on its mother's back and a baby bat shelters beneath its mother's wing.

Baby shrews attach themselves to their mother in a chain, each baby holding onto the one in front with its teeth. This is called 'caravanning'. If they can't find their mother, the babies will reattach themselves to the first moving object they see.

Dangerous strangers

Sometimes, female mammals have to protect their babies from an adult male of their own **species**. Female lions, called lionesses, often have to do this. The dangerous male is not usually the father. He is a stranger from outside the group who wants to get the female's attention, and will even kill her babies to do so.

Suckling

As well as protecting their babies, female mammals also feed them. Unlike reptiles or birds, all female mammals produce milk. Milk gives babies all the goodness they need to grow bigger and stronger. A female fur seal's milk is more than half fat. This helps her baby to gain weight quickly. Milk also contains **antibodies**, which the mother passes on to her baby to protect it from **germs**.

Milk is made in the mother's **mammary glands**. Some female mammals, including apes and elephants, have two mammary glands on their chests. Each one has a nipple on the end, which the baby sucks to get milk. This is called **suckling**. Mammals that give birth to larger litters have many nipples, often called teats, along the underside of their bodies.

A pig has six pairs of teats, so it can suckle up to twelve babies at the same time.

Toothless

Many baby mammals, including humans, are born without teeth. This means they can suckle from their mother without hurting her. Teeth grow once the babies are ready to start eating solid food that needs chewing.

Bringing up baby

Only their mother looks after most baby mammals. A male tiger disappears long before his cubs are born and will probably never meet them. Some parents, such as South American titi monkeys, stay together to share the workload of raising their babies. In certain **social mammals**, including elephants and dolphins, the youngsters also play an important role in looking after the babies of the group.

Young black-backed jackals help their parents out by feeding and looking after the pups.

Why does a kangaroo have a pouch?

Marsupials are mammals with **pouches**, such as kangaroos and koalas. Unlike other mammals, a female marsupial does not have a **placenta** to feed her baby inside the womb. This means that marsupials have shorter **gestation periods** than most other mammals. Their babies are born early, so they can start suckling as soon as possible.

A baby kangaroo is born after only one month's gestation period. It is blind, pink and only about 5 cm long – about the size of your thumb. Luckily, it has a good sense of smell and strong little front legs to help it climb up to the mother's pouch. Here it latches onto her teat to suckle. It stays inside the pouch for over six months.

Egg-laying mammals

Monotremes are the only mammals that lay their eggs. Like most marsupials, they live in **Australasia**. There are two kinds of monotreme – the duck-billed platypus and the echidna. A female duck-billed platypus lays two eggs, which hatch after about ten days. Like other mammals, the babies feed on milk from their mother. As she has no teats, they suck the milk from the fur around the openings of her mammary glands.

How do mammals grow up?

Baby mammals grow up at different speeds. A gorilla, like a human baby, grows up very slowly, and only starts to walk after 30–40 weeks (7–9 months). Before then, its mother carries it everywhere, and it continues to **suckle** from her for three years. Most small mammals grow up much faster. A common vole is ready to leave the nest and look after itself after only three weeks. After five to six weeks it can have babies of its own.

No more milk

When its mother stops producing milk, a baby mammal is ready to eat solid food. This process of change, from suckling to eating solid food, is called weaning. Once a baby is weaned, it must learn to find food for itself like adults do.

African wild dogs make sure that all their pups get something to eat.

From milk to meat

Some parents help to wean their youngsters. When their pups are four or five weeks old, African wild dogs feed them meat that has already been chewed and swallowed to make it softer. The meat is then brought back up, called regurgitation. By ten weeks the pups are fully weaned. At fourteen to sixteen weeks, they join their parents on hunting trips. By watching and copying the adults, the pups soon learn how to hunt for themselves.

Learning through play

Playing looks like fun, but it also teaches young mammals important skills. Young male elephants enjoy shoving and chasing each other. This helps to prepare them for more serious fights when they are grown up. Young females prefer running through tall grass and chasing imaginary enemies. This helps them learn how to escape from danger and protect their babies, when they become mothers themselves.

When a lion cub chases its mother's tail, it is learning hunting skills that will help it to survive when it grows bigger.

How do mammals find a home?

Mammals need a place to live that provides them with food and safety. Some, such as dormice, spend most of their lives in one small area. Others move around within a large home range, or **territory**. For a pack of Arctic wolves, this can cover over 40,000 square kilometres.

Moving out

Many young mammals have to find a place of their own when they grow up. After about sixteen months, a tiger cub leaves its mother and moves away. The mother can now concentrate on raising her next **litter** and will not usually spend any more time with her grown-up cubs.

Once a young adult tiger has found a place of its own, it will not usually try to return to its mother.

Leaving the herd

Most male and female mammals grow up differently from each other. Young female impalas stay and have their babies within the herd. Young males are driven out by the **dominant** male as soon as they are grown up. These outcast young males get together to form small **bachelor herds** of their own. In time, each one will try to join up with a new group of females.

Building a home

Some mammals build a permanent home where they spend all their life. European badgers dig a system of tunnels known as

a sett. One sett may be used for hundreds of years by many generations of badgers. Other mammals make temporary shelters. Every night an orang-utan builds a new nest of branches up in a tree. This means it can always stay near any food it has found.

A European badger sett may have over a hundred entrances and exits.

Rodent construction workers

North American beavers live in small family units. They use their strong teeth to gnaw through small trees and branches, which they pile up to make a dam across the river. This slows the river down to create a calm pond. The beavers then use more branches to build their home – called a lodge. Here they can bring up their young in safety.

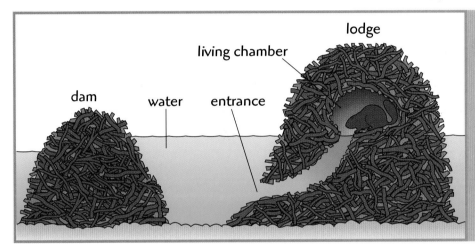

dam   water   entrance   living chamber   lodge

Beavers enter their lodge through an underwater tunnel. Inside it is warm, dry and safe from enemies.

Following food

Some mammals have to **migrate** to find their food. In east Africa, during the rainy season, blue wildebeest stay in an area where there is plenty of grass. When the dry season comes and this grass has been grazed, they migrate north to new feeding grounds. When the rains start again, they return to their original feeding area where the grass has grown back.

Blue wildebeest have to face many dangers on migration, such as fast-flowing rivers full of crocodiles.

Whale of a journey

A grey whale spends the summer in the Arctic Ocean, feeding from June to October on plankton and other tiny sea creatures. In the winter, when the ocean freezes, it migrates south down the west coast of America towards the warm waters of the **Equator**. Here, during February, its baby, or calf, is born. The calf suckles its mother's milk to grow strong enough for the long journey north again in summer.

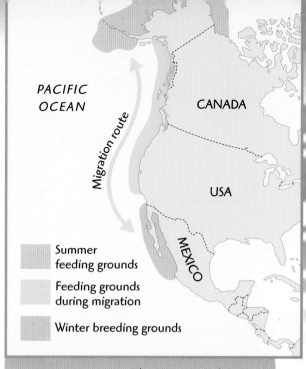

PACIFIC OCEAN

CANADA

Migration route

USA

MEXICO

Summer feeding grounds

Feeding grounds during migration

Winter breeding grounds

The 9000 km (5600 mile) migration route of the grey whale takes it up and down the west coast of North America.

A grey whale calf migrates with its mother each year. By the time it is grown up, at twelve years old, it may already have travelled over 100,000 kilometres. That is the same as swimming two and a half times around the world.

Getting along together

Living in groups provides safety in numbers for **social mammals**. Each member of a group has its own position. Usually one or two senior animals are in charge. In some mammals, such as spotted hyenas, the boss is a female. In others, such as chimpanzees, it is a male. Members of a group communicate with each other by sign language, not words.

Just like people, chimpanzees use their faces to show each other how they feel.

Moving up in the world

As social mammals grow older, the position of each individual in the group changes. There may be more than 50 baboons in one troop. Each one holds a different position. Once a female baboon has had many babies, she gains more respect from the others. Now younger females will groom her (make her neat and clean) and help look after her babies.

When do mammals have babies?

Once mammals have grown up, they are ready to start **breeding**. This means that males must get together with females to have babies. The **breeding season** is usually in spring, when there is plenty of food available for mothers and babies to stay fit and healthy.

Staking a claim

In the breeding season, a male mammal marks out his breeding **territory**. This lets females know he is there, and warns rival males to keep away. Some use scent – a male rhino leaves big smelly piles of dung beside his trails. Some make visible marks – a male leopard scratches a tree trunk with his claws. Some use sound – the song of a male humpback whale can carry for many kilometres underwater.

A male klipspringer marking his territory. He is wiping a sticky, scented liquid, from a gland at the corner of his eye, onto a twig.

Fighting bull elephant seals have fierce battles with each other. Fortunately, their skin and blubber are so thick that they do not usually cause serious injuries.

Coming to blows

Males compete with each other for ownership of a territory. Usually, showing off their size or strength is enough to avoid a fight. A male walrus with smaller tusks will not challenge one with big tusks. Sometimes, though, fights do break out. Two male bighorn sheep will crash their horns together with massive blows to see who is the stronger. Fighting giraffes will swing their heads like sledgehammers – each one trying to knock the other off balance.

Ganging up

Sometimes young males gang up to claim a territory. Two or three young male lions, working together, can force the older, **dominant** male out of the pride (family group) and take his place. Fights between male lions are so vicious that the loser is sometimes badly injured or even killed.

Mating

Female mammals usually choose to mate with the biggest and strongest males. This means that their babies will probably be big and strong. Other weaker males must wait their turn until they are bigger or older. When a female is ready for mating, she is said to be 'on heat'. A male can detect this by smelling her urine (wee). He follows her until she allows him to mate.

A pair of mating lions will stay close together for a few days.

A male and female porcupine, like these North American porcupines, stay together for life to help rear their young.

How many partners?

Some mammals stay with their partners for life. A pair of African porcupines will not separate until one of them dies. They raise many **litters** together, with both parents helping to bring up the babies. In other mammals, such as red deer, a male mates with many different females. This gives him a greater chance of producing fit and healthy babies, but he takes no part in their upbringing.

How long do mammals live?

The length of a mammal's life depends upon what kind of life it lives. Most mammals never reach old age in the wild. They die as soon as they can no longer find food or avoid **predators**. Animals tend to live longer in **captivity**. Here they have no enemies, and their food is provided.

Fast life or slow progress?

Many small mammals lead short, energetic lives. A female common shrew only lives for about two years, but in that short time she may have up to 30 babies. Each day she eats more than her own body weight in food just to stay alive. Unlike shrews, a female orang-utan may reach the old age of 50. But she grows up very slowly, and will probably have no more than four babies in her lifetime.

Elephants have few natural enemies, which means they can grow very old. Once their teeth are worn down, they can no longer eat, so they eventually die of starvation.

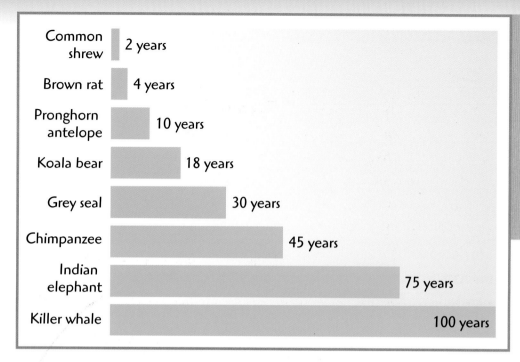

Common shrew	2 years
Brown rat	4 years
Pronghorn antelope	10 years
Koala bear	18 years
Grey seal	30 years
Chimpanzee	45 years
Indian elephant	75 years
Killer whale	100 years

This graph shows the typical life spans of different mammals that make it to adulthood.

For richer or for poorer

People are among the longest-lived of all mammals. But human life expectancy (how long someone is expected to live) depends upon how much food, water and health care people have. Today, in most of Europe and the USA, life expectancy is over 75 years for men and nearly 80 years for women. In many poor parts of Africa, though, life expectancy is less than 40 years.

Most people can expect to reach old age in countries such as the USA or Britain, where they receive plenty of food, medicine and care.

Mammals in danger

Today, many mammals are threatened with **extinction** because of people. Some, such as tigers and rhinos, are hunted to make money. Others, such as orang-utans and lemurs, have had the places where they live damaged or destroyed. We humans must try harder to look after the world so that these mammals don't disappear for ever.

The golden bamboo lemur is one of the rarest mammals in the world. Today, there are no more than 500 remaining in the wild.

The cycle of life

No mammal lives for ever. Even so, by the time an adult mammal dies, it will have helped bring many babies into the world. Not all the babies survive, but some will grow up to have babies of their own. This is the cycle of life – from birth to adulthood – in which young are born, grow and have young themselves. The cycle of life ensures the survival of each mammal **species**.

Fact file

What is ...

- **the longest gestation period?**

The African elephant has a **gestation period** of 22 months, the longest of any animal.

- **...and the shortest?**

The American opossum and the rare water opossum of central and northern South America both have the shortest gestation periods of between 12 and 13 days. These are both **marsupials**.

- **the biggest litter?**

The common tenrec, a hedgehog-like mammal from Madagascar, can have up to 32 babies in one **litter**.

- **the biggest baby?**

A new-born blue whale calf is about eight metres long and weighs two and a half tonnes. This makes it the biggest baby in the world.

- **the longest living mammal?**

Nobody knows how long the oldest mammal has lived for. The oldest recorded person was Jeanne Calment of France, who died in 1997 at the age of 122. Some species of whale, including killer whales and blue whales, can also live for over 100 years.

- **the rarest mammal?**

The Javan rhinoceros of Indonesia is one of the rarest mammals in the world. There are fewer than 100 remaining in the wild.

Can male mammals produce milk?

The dayak fruit bat of Borneo is the only species of mammal in which the males can produce milk to suckle his young.

Mammal classification

Classification is the way scientists group living things together according to features they have in common. Mammals are divided into three main groups according to how they have their young.

1. Placental mammals

These are mammals whose babies develop inside the mother's body and get food and oxygen from her **placenta** until they are born. There are about 4400 different species of placental mammal. They are divided into several smaller groups, including:

- *Carnivores:* mammals with sharp claws and teeth for hunting and eating meat, such as cats, dogs, bears and badgers.
- *Sea mammals:* mammals that live in the sea, with fins or flippers for swimming, such as whales, dolphins, seals and sea lions.
- *Primates:* mammals with well-developed hands for climbing and holding things, such as monkeys, apes, lemurs and people.
- *Ungulates:* plant-eating mammals with hooves, such as rhinos, horses, camels, cattle, deer, antelope and pigs. Elephants are also ungulates.
- *Rodents:* small mammals with strong front teeth for gnawing grain and plants, such as rats, mice and squirrels.
- *Insectivores:* small mammals that eat insects, such as hedgehogs, shrews and moles.
- *Bats:* mammals with wings, which feed on fruit or catch insects in the air.

2. Marsupials

Marsupials are mammals whose young are born very early and then climb up into a pouch on their mother's body, where they grow and develop. There are about 290 species of marsupial, including kangaroos, koalas, wombats and opossums.

3. Monotremes

Monotremes are mammals that lay eggs. They include only the duck-billed platypus and the echidna.

Glossary

antibody something in the blood that fights germs inside the body

Australasia part of the world that includes Australia, New Zealand and New Guinea

bachelor herd group of male animals that stay together until they are ready to breed

breeding having babies

breeding season special time of year when a species breeds

camouflage colour or pattern that helps an animal blend in with its background

captivity being kept in a zoo or cage, unable to get out

dominant more important or powerful than others

endothermic getting heat from inside the body

endoskeleton skeleton of bones inside an animal's body

Equator imaginary line around the centre of the Earth that divides the north from the south

extinction dying out of an animal or plant species when there is none left on Earth

fertilized when an egg is fertilized, an embryo begins to grow

foetus baby animal developing inside its mother

germs tiny life-forms that can get inside a body to cause disease

gestation period time between fertilization and birth, when a baby animal is developing

litter group of babies born at the same time to one mother

lung inflatable sac inside the body that holds air, allowing an animal to breathe

mammary gland part of a female mammal that produces milk

marsupial mammal with a pouch, such as a kangaroo

migrate/migration journey of animals from one place to another to find food or a good place for breeding

oxygen gas in the air that animals need for breathing

placenta part of a female mammal that passes food and oxygen through the blood to the unborn baby

pouch fold of skin, like a pocket, on the front of a marsupial mother's body

predator animal that hunts or catches other animals to eat them

prey animals that are hunted or caught for food by predators

rainforest thick forests of tall trees that grow in hot, sunny places where it rains almost every day

skull bones inside the head that protect the brain

social mammals mammals that live together in groups

species unique type of animal. Males and females of the same species can breed to produce healthy offspring.

sperm seed produced in the body of a male animal used to fertilize the eggs of a female

suckle/suckling drinking milk from a mother

territory area that an animal claims as its own for feeding or breeding

Find out more

Books

1000 Things You Should Know About Mammals, Duncan Brewer (Miles Kelly Publishing, 2002)

Eyewitness: Mammals, Steve Parker (Dorling Kindersley, 1989)

Eye Wonder: Mammals, Sarah Walker (Dorling Kindersley, 2002)

Life Cycles of Cats and other Mammals, Sally Morgan (Belitha Press, 2001)

Questions and Answers: Mammals, Barbara Taylor (Kingfisher, 2002)

Question Time: Mammals, Jim Bruce (Larousse Kingfisher Chambers, 2001)

Websites

The Kidscom site – lots of fun games to learn about animals:
http://www.kidscom.com/games/animal/animal.html

The Scholastic site – fun animal facts:
http://www.kidzone.ws/animals/mammals.htm

The Enchanted Learning site – curriculum-led fun and facts
http://www.AllAboutMammals.com

The International Wildlife Rehabilitation Council site:
http://www.iwrc-online.org/kids/Facts/Mammals/mammals.htm

The Cyber Sleuth Kids search engine – for lots of sites about animals:
http://cybersleuth-kids.com/sleuth/Science/Animals/Mammals/index.htm

The Worldwide Fund for Nature site:
http://www.wwf-uk.org

Index

African wild dogs 15, 16

baby mammals 4, 5–16, 28
badgers 18, 29
bats 4, 28, 29
beavers 19
breeding 22–24

camouflage 10
chimpanzees 21
classification 29
communication 21
dolphins 8, 13, 29
duck-billed platypus 14, 29

eggs 5, 14
elephants 5, 6, 12, 13, 16,
    25, 28, 29
extinction 27

food and feeding 12, 13, 14,
    15–16, 19, 20, 25, 29

gestation periods 5, 14, 28
giraffes 9, 10, 23
gorillas 15
groups and herds 6, 18, 21
growth 15

hedgehogs 7, 29
homes 17–19
humans 4, 9, 26, 29

kangaroos 11, 14, 29

lemmings 8
life spans 25–26, 28
lions 11, 16, 23, 24

marsupials 14, 28, 29
migration 19, 20
milk 4, 12, 14, 15, 20, 28
monotremes 14, 29

orang-utans 25, 27

pangolins 4
placental mammals 5, 7, 29
play 16
porcupines 24
predators 7, 9, 11, 25

rhinos 7, 22, 27, 28, 29

seals 23
shrews 11, 25, 29
social mammals 6, 13, 21
species of mammal 4
suckling 12, 13, 14, 15, 20, 28

tapirs 10
territories 17, 22, 23
tigers 13, 17, 27

verterbrates 4

whales 4, 20, 22, 28, 29
wildebeest 19